THE

VIOLENT RISE

OF ISIS

THE CRIMES OF ISIS

The VIOLENT RISE of ISIS

Chris Townsend

Enslow Publishing
101 W. 23rd Street
Suite 240
New York, NY 10011
USA

enslow.com

Published in 2018 by Enslow Publishing, LLC.
101 W. 23rd Street, Suite 240, New York, NY 10011

Library of Congress Cataloging-in-Publication Data

Names: Townsend, Chris, author.
Title: The violent rise of ISIS / by Chris Townsend.
Description: New York : Enslow Publishing, 2018. | Series: The crimes of ISIS
| Includes bibliographical references and index. | Audience: Grades 7–12.
Identifiers: LCCN 2017026286 | ISBN 9780766092105 (library bound) | ISBN
9780766095793 (paperback)
Subjects: LCSH: IS (Organization)—Juvenile literature. | Middle
East—History—21st century—Juvenile literature. | Terrorism—Religious
aspects—Islam—Juvenile literature. | Islamic
fundamentalism—History—Juvenile literature.
Classification: LCC HV6433.I722 T698 2018 | DDC 363.3250956—dc23
LC record available at https://lccn.loc.gov/2017026286

Printed in the United States of America

To Our Readers: We have done our best to make sure all website addresses in this
book were active and appropriate when we went to press. However, the author and
the publisher have no control over and assume no liability for the material available on
those websites or on any websites they may link to. Any comments or suggestions can
be sent by email to customerservice@enslow.com.

Photo Credits: Cover, p. 3 Gokhan Sahin/Getty Images; p. 6 Christophe Simon/
AFP/Getty Images; pp. 8–9 Sebastiano Tomada/Getty Images; pp. 11, 36–37 © AP
Images; p. 14 CNN/3rd Party-Misc/Getty Images; p. 16 Hurriyet/AP Images; p. 19
Mohammad Hannon/AP Images; p. 23 Dia Hamid/AFP/Getty Images; pp. 24–
25 Karim Sahib/AFP/Getty Images; p. 29 U.S. Army/Getty Images; pp. 32–33
The Washington Post/Getty Images; pp. 40–41 Bilal Fawzi/AP Images; p. 43,
78, 86–87 NurPhoto/Getty Images; pp. 46–47 JM Lopez/AFP/Getty Images; p. 51
Mir Hamid/Daily Dawn/Gamma-Rapho/Getty Images; p. 52 Francis Dean/Corbis
Historical/Getty Images; pp. 54–55 Delil Souleiman/AFP/Getty Images; p. 58
Banaras Khan/AFP/Getty Images; pp. 61, 62 Philip Ojisua/AFP/Getty Images;
pp. 66–67 Anadolu Agency/Getty Images; pp. 70–71 Bay Ismoyo/AFP/Getty
Images; pp. 74–75 Saleh Al-Obeidi/AFP/Getty Images; p. 80 Dan Kitwood/Getty
Images; pp. 82–83 Martyn Aim/Getty Images.

CONTENTS

Members of Iraq's Counter Terrorism Service and Emergency Response Division patrol a street in Mosul, Iraq, during the 2017 battle to retake the city from ISIS. The Iraqis have been fighting a continuous ground war against ISIS since the group's seemingly sudden and very violent rise in 2014.

INTRODUCTION

On July 5, 2014, after the stunning seizure of Mosul, Iraq, a relatively unknown man in black stepped into an Iraqi mosque and declared that the Islamic State of Iraq and Syria, or ISIS, had reestablished the caliphate, an Islamic body of governance not seen since the early days of the religion. Large swathes of Iraq and Syria have been swept under a medieval wave of violence. Other groups as far away as Nigeria and Indonesia have also pledged loyalty to the group, waging their own campaigns of violence. From the beginning, the rise of ISIS has been a violent one.

In the wilds of Afghanistan, a bloody seed took root. Shaped by a decade of violence, a group of fighters would establish a base from which to challenge the world order. These fighters pledged themselves to an idea more than a thousand years old. Early in its history, Islam dominated much of the world. These fighters sought to restore this caliphate of old. They set about achieving their goal with vicious attacks against anyone they deemed a threat. As the group grew, its influence spread from

Iraqi security forces approach a vehicle that was destroyed during fighting with ISIS in June 2014. Following a decade of war with the United States, Iraq was left unstable, leaving room for ISIS to rise up.

rural Afghanistan. On September 11, 2001, the group, known as al-Qaeda, struck out at a giant, the United States. Thousands of Americans died. The attack would plunge the Middle East into war once more.

In the chaos, a new group rose to claim the mantle of the caliphate, and ISIS was born. Its violence and brutality would exceed anything that had been seen before. Its attacks against

even others of its faith and its extreme level of violence would lead to its exile from its parent organization. Undeterred, ISIS began to build its empire in the deserts of Syria and Iraq. The group seized several towns and forced those who could not manage to flee to live under medieval Islamic laws.

Controlling land, ISIS had what no jihadist terrorist group had possessed since the banning of the caliphate more than a hundred ago. The leader of ISIS declared himself caliph, the leader of all the world's Muslims. Every Muslim was told to come fight for ISIS or kill infidels in their own lands. A surprisingly sophisticated propaganda and recruiting campaign was waged online for the heart and soul of the Muslim community. Thousands came to fight. Thousands more died.

As the danger expanded, threatening to cover the world with ISIS's dark vision for the future, the world pushed back. A coalition of nations that includes military forces in Syria and Iraq has begun to drive ISIS from its lands. Even without its physical territory, though, ISIS will remain a threat unless the world can overcome the conditions that allowed the group to rise to such prominence. ISIS was born in violence. It has created an environment full of violence. It will meet its end in violence. But more than violence is needed to finally put the evil ideology that inspired the group to rest. ISIS rose to power through a never-before-seen campaign of violence, but everything that rises must fall. The violent rise of ISIS is nearing its end.

1

ROOTS OF

EVIL

No group springs wholly formed from the air. Groups like ISIS are descended from and have been shaped by the groups from which they evolved. International aggression and meddling played a part in the group's rise and created an army of holy warriors. Given a safe space to plan and grow, these holy warriors would seek to remake the world according to their dark vision.

THE RUSSIAN DEBACLE

The roots of the Islamic State can be found in the rugged mountains and flowering fields of Afghanistan. During an extended conflict between the Communist government and various Afghan insurgencies, the Soviet Union sent troops and tanks across the border to shore up its failing partner. Thirty thousand Soviet troops flowed into the country, trampling the colorful fields of poppies.

Soviet forces were immediately attacked by tribal forces during the invasion of Afghanistan. The Soviets responded by sending more than 100,000 extra troops into the country to occupy the cities. A Palestinian scholar and preacher in Jordan, Abdullah Azzam, wrote what would become the founding document of a resistance movement. His paper was called "The Defense of Muslim Lands, the First Obligation After Faith."[1] Azzam's fatwa, or religious decree, declared that the presence of Soviets in Muslim lands was cause for jihad, or holy war. All able-bodied Muslims were supposed to leave their lands and come to the defense of their brethren in Afghanistan. Tens of thousands of jihadists flowed from around the world to fight against the Soviets.[2] It was an opportunity that the United States could not resist.

The modern roots of ISIS can be traced back to the mujahideen of Afghanistan in the 1980s. The mujahideen fought the Soviets in part, they believed, to defend Islam from the West.

FLOWERING FIELDS

The poppies of Afghanistan have been the source of billions of dollars for those who control these wild lands.[3] The sap from the poppy flowers can be dried and made into opium, morphine, and heroin. Before the Soviet invasion of Afghanistan, production was limited. The United States has been accused of creating the booming market that still stands today in its efforts to raise money to support anti-Soviet forces.[3] As the mujahideen, or holy warriors, tightened their grip on Afghanistan, they expanded the market even further by requiring farmers to plant more poppies. By 2016, opium produced from Afghan poppies totaled nearly 5,000 tons, which would potentially yield billions of dollars for the production chain, including the terrorist groups that run the poppy fields.[5] It is a strange crop for a group that claims to represent the holiest and most correct version of its faith.

The United States and the Soviet Union had been enemies since the end of World War II. While direct war was avoided, over the years, various conflicts between the United States and Communist forces in Korea and Vietnam had left a scar on American honor. Afghanistan presented an opportunity to further destabilize the crumbling Soviet Union. The United States began providing weapons and training to the mujahideen of Afghanistan. Among the American-backed forces was a tall, thin Saudi named Osama bin Laden. The United States would have occasion later to regret its support for the fierce yet lanky holy warrior.

The Soviet Union was defeated and soon collapsed under the weight of its social and economic problems. The mujahideen had taken down an empire. American support dried up with its only real interest in the conflict defeated. The seeds had been sown for the growth of a global jihad from the wilds of Afghanistan. A generation of Muslim warriors, hardened by a decade of conflict, turned its gaze outward. They formed a group called al-Qaeda ("the base" in Arabic). After successfully defending the Muslims of Afghanistan, the group decided it should defend Muslims everywhere and unite them under a global caliphate.

HOLY WARRIORS

The mujahideen of Afghanistan came from all walks of life. Osama bin Laden was an educated son of a wealthy family. Though trained as a civil engineer, he responded to Azzam's call to jihad and found his way to Afghanistan. His father was a rich businessman in Saudi Arabia, giving the young jihadist access to significant sums of money. Bin Laden's efforts in Afghanistan largely focused on financing, recruiting, and training the fighters pouring in from around the world. Bin Laden would bring Azzam to neighboring Pakistan and set up a recruiting center and propaganda office. As the war with the Soviet Union dragged on, the various factions of mujahideen began fighting among themselves.

In 1988, bin Laden formally established his group, al-Qaeda, to unite the jihadists under a common banner. After the Soviet withdrawal from Afghanistan, bin Laden continued to grow his group. But the insurgency and its fighters faced a challenge after Soviet withdrawal from Afghanistan. The reason most had come was to fight the foreign invader in Muslim lands. The Soviet troops were gone. The puppet government they left in their wake and continued to support from afar was a source of angst, but not the motivator that actual Soviet troops had been.

CNN EXCLUSIVE

This clip from 1998 shows Osama bin Laden (*center*), the leader of al-Qaeda, talking with Ayman al-Zawahiri (*left*), who is the current leader of al-Qaeda. Although bin Laden condemned ISIS for its treatment of Muslims, Zawahiri has sometimes been an ally of the group.

In 1992, Afghanistan's Communist government collapsed without its Soviet backer. The Islamic State of Afghanistan was established as the formal government for the embattled country.[6] As the dust of a decade of war settled, a religious theocracy rose to seize power in Afghanistan. They called themselves the Taliban, meaning "students" in Pashto (one of Afghanistan's official languages). The Taliban seized power in 1996 and quickly enforced Islamic laws. It was a harbinger for things to come. The Taliban provided a haven in the mountains of Afghanistan from which bin Laden and his group could continue their growth and planning.

A SAFE SPACE

Deep in Afghanistan in the city of Kandahar there lies a mosque. Beside the mosque is a shrine. Three padlocks of different sizes bar the entrance. Inside lies a table loaded with Qurans that one must pass under to reach yet another door with three locks. Within the innermost sanctum of the shrine is a silver chest. It is locked in a chest that is, in turn, locked in another chest. Deep in the innermost chest is a cloak that is said to have been worn by the Prophet Muhammad, the founder of Islam. The keepers of the chest were chosen in a secret ceremony where participants took turns shouting "Allahu Akbar" ("God is Great") until the lock magically opened. Legend says that whoever can open the chest and wear the cloak is the leader of all Muslims. It is the stuff of fairy tales. For Mullah Muhamad Omar, leader of the Taliban, the cloak would cement his status as the rightful ruler of Afghanistan. In 1996, after the Taliban seized power, he took the cloak to the top of the nearby mosque and held it over his head with his hands in the sleeves of the cloak.[7] The whole of Afghanistan would soon belong to the Taliban.

The Taliban quickly established a government and a series of courts consistent with Islamic law and the traditions of the Prophet and the earliest Muslims. Men were required to be bearded. Women had to cover themselves from head to toe. Music and dancing were forbidden. Bin Laden and al-Qaeda were promised safe haven so long as they did not attack the United States. The group seized the opportunity and the protection it offered to begin expanding its network of fighters and training camps. But despite its promise, from the mountains and caves of Afghanistan the leaders of al-Qaeda began to plot their attack against the far enemy, the United States.

The group began to spread. Offshoots of al-Qaeda began to appear around the world. After a series of attacks against

American interests, al-Qaeda carried out the largest terrorist attack in history. Members of the group hijacked four planes on September 11, 2001. Two of the planes flew into the Twin Towers of the World Trade Center in New York City. A third plane crashed into the side of the Pentagon outside Washington, DC. On hearing the fate of the other three planes, the passengers of the fourth attacked their hijackers and their plane crashed into a field in Shanksville, Pennsylvania. America's response would be swift.

As America and its allies turned their full attention on the wayward Afghanistan, the country's leadership disintegrated. Al-Qaeda and the Taliban melted into the countryside, many taking refuge in neighboring Pakistan. Despite sustaining a

Taliban fighters are shown near Kabul, Afghanistan, in 1996. The Taliban is an Islamic fundamentalist group that has helped to inspire the leaders of ISIS.

SHOCK AND AWE

Less than a month after the attacks of September 11, 2001, the night sky of Afghanistan lit up like midday. The United States had demanded that the Taliban close all terror camps and turn over bin Laden to answer for his crimes. The Taliban's refusal to hand over the terrorist leader, despite its disagreement with his actions, was the last straw. Fifteen bombers, twenty-five fighter jets, and fifty missiles fired from ships and subs at sea decimated Taliban and al-Qaeda military capabilities. The strike lasted six hours, continuously pounding targets on the ground.[8] Sensitive to the potential for a humanitarian crisis as the government was dismantled, the United States also dropped pallets of meals ready to eat in rural areas. As the dust settled, Special Operations forces went to work in the hills and valleys of Afghanistan. It would prove to be a fatal blow for Taliban rule in Afghanistan.

mortal blow, al-Qaeda was not yet dead. The seeds it had sown in faraway countries were beginning to bear fruit. From a prison in Jordan, a leader would rise and continue the work of al-Qaeda. Hardened by the conflicts in Afghanistan and his efforts at home, the man would start his own organization. The work would continue, but the focus shifted. Not content to wait for the natural rising of a caliphate, he would seek to impose one. The caliphate would rise anew from the deserts of Iraq, with its eyes set on global domination.

2

BRANCHING
OUT

Al-Qaeda was bent on world domination, but it wasn't in any hurry. Osama bin Laden thought that the caliphate would arise naturally from the Muslim population once he and his group created the right conditions. In Jordan, one recruit had different plans. He would not content himself with the focus on faraway enemies. He would not wait for a caliphate. He would impose one.

RISING STAR

No one expected that Abu Musab al-Zarqawi would ever make much of himself. Tattooed and fond of drinking and gambling, as a young man, Zarqawi was suspected of running a prostitution ring.[1] At twenty-three, Zarqawi answered the call to jihad in Afghanistan and trained at one of Azzam's training camps. In Afghanistan, Zarqawi would discover his purpose in life. He met a mentor, Sheikh Abu Muhammad al-Maqdisi, who would be instrumental in shaping the ideology of his student. Zarqawi left Afghanistan and returned with Maqdisi to Jordan, intent on restoring the caliphate.

In Jordan, Zarqawi and Maqdisi ran afoul of the government. They were planning a bombing campaign. When it was discovered, the two were sentenced to prison. It was in prison that Zarqawi truly came into his own. While Maqdisi was the scholar, Zarqawi was the enforcer and leader. In prison he assembled a loyal group of followers. Zarqawi memorized the entire Quran and began to enforce Islamic law in the prison. In an extreme act of penance for his prior life, Zarqawi smuggled a razor blade into prison and cut off his tattoos, slicing the offensive skin from his body.[2]

Abu Qatada (*center*), an al-Qaeda-linked preacher, talks with Abu Muhammad al-Maqdisi (*left*), the spiritual leader who helped inspire ISIS founder Abu Musab al-Zarqawi.

PIOUS FOREFATHERS

Maqdisi was a scholar in the Salafi tradition of Sunni Islam. Salafis believe in a very narrow interpretation of Islamic scripture and believe that everyone should live the way that the Prophet and the early Muslims lived nearly 1,500 years ago. Salafis shun the modern world and all its trappings. While the Quran is the basis for the ideology, Salafism places a lot of importance on other sources, such as the sunna and the hadith. The sunna is a collection of stories about the life and behavior of the prophet Muhammad. The hadith is a collection of the Prophet's sayings.

Muhammad is considered the most perfect Muslim. Anything that he did is considered the best way to do things. From the way he wore his beard and pants, to the way he drank his water, Salafists follow his example in all things. Piety and adherence to the purest form of Islam are central to the ideology. Innovation is forbidden, as it would suggest that Islam as practiced by the early Muslims was not already perfect. Any Muslim who does not live up to the high standards of Salafists can be deemed an infidel. Once a Muslim is declared an infidel, he can be killed. Labeling someone an infidel, a process called *takfir*, is a death sentence. It is the most dangerous aspect of the ideology because it allows the group to kill anyone it wants.

Zarqawi left prison a famous man. When he returned to Afghanistan, he was granted an audience with Osama bin Laden. The two disagreed about whether to focus on the near enemy, corrupt Arab leaders, or the far enemy, the United States. Then the United States invaded Afghanistan following the attacks on September 11, 2001. As al-Qaeda lost its support base and had to go into hiding, it was necessary for the group to branch out. Bin Laden gave Zarqawi $5,000 to establish an al-Qaeda affiliate. Zarqawi then went to a training camp in Iraq. There he formed a group named Unity and Jihad, renaming the group after pledging allegiance to bin Laden as al-Qaeda in Iraq (AQI).

However, disagreements between bin Laden and Zarqawi would continue to be a source of problems. Zarqawi was extremely violent and had no qualms about killing other Muslims. Zarqawi was still a very low-level player in the organization. The United States would change that when it invaded Iraq, naming Zarqawi as a key link between Saddam Hussein and terrorist organizations.[3]

FIRST STRIKES

Laurence Foley had devoted his life to helping others. As an American diplomat working with the United States Agency for International Development in Jordan, he helped provide clean drinking water, improved medical clinics, and assisted entrepreneurs with establishing new businesses. The American embassy always reminds workers to vary their schedules. Being unpredictable makes it harder for terrorists to target employees in their daily tasks. On the morning of October 28, 2002, Foley headed out to his Mercedes with its telltale diplomatic plates. He had recently received an award for his work with the Jordanian people. The night before, he had told his wife, "I am where I want to be, doing what I want to do."[4]

As he approached his vehicle, a man came out of the bushes on the far side of the car. The man shot Foley eight times and fled. Laurence Foley was dead. An investigation found the shooter and his accomplices. They confessed to the crime. They told investigators that Zarqawi had ordered the hit as an attack against America. The attack supported the American assertion that Zarqawi was working in nearby Iraq under the protection of dictator Saddam Hussein. It would prove to be the final nail in Saddam's coffin. A few months later, American forces entered Iraq.

With the Americans entering Iraq, Zarqawi redoubled his efforts to sow chaos around the foreign forces. He bombed the Jordanian embassy in Baghdad in August 2003. Several days later, he attacked the nearby United Nations headquarters, killing nearly two dozen people. Attacking Westerners was part of Zarqawi's strategy, but he had even bigger plans. Zarqawi wanted to cause outright civil war between the Sunni and Shia factions in Iraq. Sinking the country into a civil war around the American forces would be a huge victory. August would end on an even bloodier note. Zarqawi sent car bombers to a Shia shrine in Najaf. When the bombs exploded, they killed more than a hundred people. Iraq descended into chaos, just like Zarqawi hoped.

The level of violence exploded as Shias began to attack Sunnis as revenge for the continuing attacks on Shia holy sites. American forces found themselves hopelessly bogged down in a sectarian conflict where they were often the target of both sides. Zarqawi was not done. In 2004, the violence reached a horrifying new level that would become the new norm. Zarqawi released a video wherein he beheaded an American businessman, Nick Berg. Behind him on the wall was the now-infamous black flag with its declaration of faith. It would come to be known as the flag of ISIS.

Construction workers outside Iraq's Ali al-Hadi shrine mosque work to help repair damage caused by al-Qaeda when the group blew up the mosque and took down its famed golden dome.

DISTURBING THE BASE

Zarqawi's excessive use of violence, especially against other Muslims, was beginning to draw condemnation from al-Qaeda. Zarqawi sent suicide bombers to a wedding in Jordan, killing sixty Muslims. Bin Laden was reportedly furious.[5] Bin Laden's second-in-command, Zawahiri, sent a letter to Zarqawi asking him to tone down the violence and the attacks on Muslims. Zarqawi ignored the letter and continued his campaign of violence. Despite his pledge of loyalty to al-Qaeda, his group was becoming a force in its own right. The timid sheikhs hiding in Afghan caves couldn't control Zarqawi. The spark that bin Laden had encouraged in Iraq had become an inferno that no one controlled except Zarqawi.

In April 2006, Zarqawi released a bold new video proclaiming himself the leader of al-Qaeda in Iraq and promising to establish an Islamic State. Unknown to Zarqawi, treachery was afoot. One of his soldiers, perhaps out of a sense of loyalty to bin Laden, gave American forces information on one of Zarqawi's closest advisors. That tip led the American military to Zarqawi's safe house in Baquba, Iraq. Two F-16 fighter jets were scrambled, each carrying 500-pound bombs. As Zarqawi met with his advisors, the two bombs found their target. Zarqawi and five other terrorists were pulled from the rubble, dead. Zarqawi's body was instantly recognizable from the scars left behind by his gruesome tattoo removal.[6]

Zarqawi was dead and with him al-Qaeda in Iraq. The victory, however, would be short-lived. The remnants of his organization quickly reformed as the Islamic State in

A young man reads an Iraqi newspaper reporting on the death of Abu Musab al-Zarqawi, the leader of al-Qaeda in Iraq, the precursor to the Islamic State.

THE GOLDEN MOSQUE

The al-Askari Mosque in Samarra, Iraq, with its golden dome and minarets, was one of the most important sites for Shia pilgrims. The tenth and eleventh imams were buried there. The legendary twelfth imam was supposedly taken from Earth by God on that site. Shia lore holds that this twelfth, or hidden, imam, will return to Earth in the last days. Thousands came from all over Iraq and Iran each year to visit the holy site. Only the shrines to Muhammad's son-in-law, Ali, and grandson, Husayn, in Najaf and Karballah, respectively, are more sacred to Shia Muslims.

On February 22, 2006, several men entered the mosque wearing Iraqi army uniforms. After they left, two bombs exploded. The golden dome of the mosque collapsed into the building. The Shia were outraged, and their response was swift and violent. By some reports, more than three thousand people were killed in the chaos that followed, as Sunni mosques and imams were attacked.[7] A little more than a year later, the mosque was bombed again, destroying the golden minarets. Any chance of preventing the slide into sectarian war in Iraq lay in the rubble of the once-great mosque.

Iraq. Zarqawi's violent vision would continue under new management. Divorced from al-Qaeda, the new organization would go about establishing the caliphate and a global Islamic State. As America shifted tactics and began using Sunni forces to combat extremism in western Iraq, the Islamic State kept to the shadows.

Political upheavals over the next few years, and the withdrawal of American forces from Iraq, would be all the tinder needed to turn the glowing embers of the terrorist organization into a raging fire once more. Seizing the opportunity, the group would expand across Syria and Iraq until the group's new leader stepped up to the pulpit in Mosul and declared the reestablishment of the caliphate under the flag of the Islamic State of Iraq and Syria, or ISIS.

3

SPRING

GROWTH

With its powerful and charismatic leader dead, al-Qaeda in Iraq (AQI) was facing a crisis. The appointment of an Egyptian bomb maker, Abu Ayab al-Masri, as the new leader did little to help keep a local face on the franchise. The group was losing momentum. It was reduced to stirring up sectarian violence between the Sunni and Shia people in Iraq. Al-Masri announced a new group headed by an Iraqi, Abu Umar al-Baghdadi. He called the new group the Islamic State in Iraq (ISI).

EVOLUTION

In 2007, the sectarian violence was out of control. Sunni insurgents, many of them aligned with the Islamic State in Iraq, were attacking Shia sites and villages. Shia militias were striking back. The Iraqi government was bogged down with its own troubles and was not respected by many Iraqis. Water, gas, and electricity were rare luxuries unavailable to many of the country's citizens. On an average day in the capital city, there were fifty attacks and three car bombs.[1] Caught in the midst of the escalating violence were ten thousand American troops. President George W. Bush, on the advice of General David Petraeus, increased the number of US troops to thirty thousand. The effort became known as the Surge. The military established outposts all over Baghdad and in the surrounding towns to improve security. They provided training and equipment to Sunni tribes in western Iraq who wanted to cast out their jihadist infiltrators. In 2007, the tide began to turn. Security improved. Attacks decreased. There was hope that the divisions in Iraqi society might be resolved through good governance. Thousands of jihadists had been killed or captured. The Americans began the slow process of reducing troop levels toward an eventual withdrawal as a new president promised to end the war.

US president Barack Obama speaks with US Army general David Petraeus during a helicpoter tour over Iraq in 2008. Petraeus led American involvement in Iraq in 2007 and 2008.

GOING HOME

President Barack Obama, while supportive of US efforts in Afghanistan after the September 11, 2001, attacks, had always opposed the invasion of Iraq. One of his campaign promises had been to end the "bad war" in Iraq to focus on winning the "good war" in Afghanistan.[2] True to his word, troop levels in Iraq dropped dramatically after he took office in 2009. American forces were ordered to end combat operations and withdraw by the end of 2011. The biggest point of contention was the lack of an agreement to protect American forces from local prosecution in Iraq. On December 18, 2011, the last American soldiers crossed the border into neighboring Kuwait. The withdrawal ended nearly a decade of military operations in the struggling country. Aside from military personnel at the embassy in Baghdad, the military was done with Iraq — at least for the time being.

One of the challenges in snatching terrorists off the street was keeping them from returning to the battle. At the height of the Surge, there were twenty-seven thousand detainees in American custody in Iraq.[3] Among the detainees were some of the worst jihadists in Iraq. The prison systems became recruiting grounds and indoctrination centers. Captured AQI and ISI zealots spread their message of global domination. In one of these camps, a leader rose. Ibrahim al-Badri was a quiet man. He had been arrested while visiting a jihadist friend in Fallujah, Iraq, but was not considered a jihadist himself. At the prison he preached sermons, settled disputes, and played soccer.[4] He was released only to reappear ten years later as the new caliph of ISIS, Abu Bakr al-Badghadi.

With American forces gone, the Iraqi government, largely dominated by Shias, began to consolidate power. It reversed many of the gains from the Surge. Sunnis once again found themselves on the sidelines with little or no government support. This was especially true in western Iraq, where the Islamic State was once again stirring. The Islamic State in Iraq began a series of operations to capitalize on Sunni anger. Its first targets were sheiks and other leaders who had helped the Americans during the 2007 Surge. Then the group turned its attention to the police and security forces, killing thousands with a series of bombings and drive-by shootings.[5] The Islamic State was growing again, but it needed more uncontrolled space within which to train, operate, and plan. In faraway Tunisia, a disgruntled fruit seller lit himself on fire. His death started a movement that would consume most of the Middle East. It toppled regimes that had stood for decades. The Islamic State would get its wish.

ARAB SPRING

The series of protests that rocked the Middle East and North Africa in 2011 is often referred to as the Arab Spring. Protests and outright revolts broke out in countries across the region. In Tunisia, long-time dictator Ben Ali was forced to flee with his family as his government collapsed. In Libya, Muammar Gaddafi was facing a rebellion from military forces in eastern Libya. As he mobilized his army to march on the enemy forces, the United States, with its partners, conducted a series of airstrikes that toppled the Libyan government and eventually led to Gaddafi's death. In Egypt, millions turned out for protests that led to the ouster and arrest of President Hosni Mubarak. In Bahrain, when protests threatened to topple the minority Sunni regime, Saudi Arabia sent tanks across the bridge to support its neighbor. Monarchs in Jordan, Morocco, and Saudi Arabia

During the Arab Spring in 2011, Libya was able to get rid of its dictatorial leader, Muammar Gaddafi. Here, Libyans are seen celebrating their victory over Gaddafi by touring his destroyed compound.

POLITICAL ISLAM

Islam has been both a religious and a political instrument since its inception. After Muhammad was driven out of Mecca in Saudi Arabia, he went to Medina, where he was the governor for several years. As governor, Muhammad used the Quran as a source of law to control the city. Many of his decisions, captured in stories and sayings, remain important to Islamists as an example of how Islam can be used as a governing system. The system is not without its critics. A purely Islamic government would govern according to sharia, or Islamic law. Any religious government risks alienating those of other faiths as it seeks to impose its own beliefs as law. Various Islamic republics have been implemented over the years, though their adherence to and imposition of Islamic law has been inconsistent. One of the primary challenges is the division within the faith. Would a global Islamic State be Sunni or Shia? ISIS represents the most extreme interpretation of political Islam. It seeks to force the entire world to live as a Sunni Islamic state, according to its version of the teachings and traditions of Muhammad.

made a series of political and social concessions to preserve their kingdoms. Seeing the fate of the dictators around him, Bashar al-Assad, the president of Syria, tightened his grip. As Syrian forces fired on protesters, the country descended into a civil war. The war would leave large swathes of Syria as ungoverned space. The stage was set for the revival of the Islamic State.

After the dramatic upheavals in the region, political parties began fighting for power. The most organized of the political parties were Islamist parties like Enehada in Tunisia and the Muslim Brotherhood in Egypt. They controlled the mosques and could easily motivate large numbers of voters to go to the polls and support their candidates. These Islamist parties often espoused ideas similar to al-Qaeda and the Islamic State, but there was a key difference: Islamist parties wanted to rise to power through nonviolent means like elections.

While initially successful, Islamist parties have not been able to maintain power. In Tunisia, the Islamist party lost the following election to less religious parties. In Egypt, the Islamist president was ousted by the military after massive protests. Ongoing squabbles between Islamist and secular fronts continue to obstruct progress in other countries. These failures provided the Islamic State with a powerful message. It believes that these cases are proof that the world will never allow Islamists to live and rule according to the tenets of their faith. ISIS would solve this problem by forcing the world to succumb to Islamic rule as a global caliphate ruled by the caliph of ISIS.

REVITALIZATION

The failure of the Arab Spring to lead to any real change for Muslims in the region was more fuel for the Islamic State. Iraq was in shambles after the American withdrawal, and there was little government control in the western part of the country. In Syria, a civil war was raging, leaving most of the eastern country ungoverned. It was in this uncontrolled space that the Islamic State in Iraq was able to consolidate its power. From the cocoon imposed by strong government and military action against the group, weakened by lack of attention and control, a grotesque creature emerged.

Seizing on the chaos around it, the Islamic State in Iraq announced its merger with al-Nusra Front, a Syrian opposition

Pro-ISIS demonstrators march in front of the offices of the provisional Iraqi government in Mosul in 2014. Although ISIS appeared to pop up out of nowhere that spring, the terror group grew out of al-Qaeda in Iraq, which first operated in Iraq in 2004.

group. The new group would be called the Islamic State in Iraq and the Sham. Sham is the Arabic name for the greater Levant region, which includes Syria, Lebanon, Jordan, and Israel/Palestine. The new name would lead to some confusion about what to call the group. The most correct English translation is the Islamic State in Iraq and the Levant (ISIL). The most common name is the Islamic State in Iraq and al-Sham (sometimes translated as Syria or Greater Syria), or ISIS. Some avoid the confusion altogether and refer to the group simply as the Islamic State (IS). Others have argued for using the Arabic acronym Da'esh, short for Dowlat al-Islamiya f-il-Iraq w-ash-Sham, to avoid referring to the group as Islamic. The irony of this assertion is that it fails to recognize that the exact translation of the Arabic name is the Islamic State in Iraq and the Levant. Some prefer the name Da'esh for its similarity to another Arabic word, *da'as*, which can mean "to crush or trample." ISIS has threatened to cut the tongue out of anyone who refers to it by that name.[6]

Regardless of the confusion over names, ISIS was now fully conceived and expanding its reach and power. In 2014, the terror group seized the Iraqi city of Mosul. The Iraqi army fled from the approaching jihadists, leaving the citizens of Mosul to their new rulers. Now that the terror group controlled a large portion of land across Syria and Iraq, it had all the trappings of an actual state.

ROTTEN

FRUIT

4

Now that ISIS controlled land, it set about establishing itself as a state. The group's leader, Abu Bakr al-Baghdadi, had risen from relative obscurity to demand the allegiance of the world's Muslims. As ISIS tightened its grip on its lands in Iraq and Syria, many fled the brutal rule of the group, but many others were trapped in ISIS-run cities. As fighters continued to pour in from around the world, the influence and strength of ISIS grew in the region.

COMMANDER OF THE BELIEVERS

Abu Bakr al-Baghdadi launched to infamy from the pulpit of the mosque in Mosul. His mannerisms and behavior might have seemed strange to someone unfamiliar with Islamic history. First, he was dressed all in black. William McCants, the author of *The ISIS Apocalypse*, believes that this was an attempt to associate ISIS with the great caliphates of Islam's past, especially its battles against infidels.[1]

39

In 2013, protesters wave pro-Islamist flags during an antigovernment rally in Fallujah, Iraq. The Sunni Islamist protesters would help pave the way for the rise of ISIS.

THE GOLDEN AGE

For nearly five hundred years, the Abbasid caliphate, from its capitol in Baghdad, Iraq, was the center of the learned world. Beginning in the eighth century CE, the caliph Harun ar-Rashid created the House of Wisdom. The main purpose for the new effort was to translate all of the world's knowledge into Arabic and create a grand library. Without these translations it is possible that none of the great works of science and philosophy from Greece and Rome would have survived. Without the Golden Age of Islam, the Renaissance in Europe, which lifted the world from the Dark Ages, might not have happened at all. Anyone who wanted to learn about the arts or sciences went to Baghdad to train.

Significant progress was made in mathematics. The Arabs invented the concept of zero. The word "algebra" is Arabic for "putting together broken parts into a whole." The first universities in the world were formed during this time and taught all manner of science and art. Hospitals were established where advanced surgeries, including eye surgery, were performed. Poetry, art, and the amazing architecture for which the Middle East is known all saw major advancements during the era.[2]

Sadly, the era of Arab enlightenment ended with a foreign invader. One of Genghis Khan's descendants came from the Mongol lands to the east and sacked the city. Haluga Khan destroyed most of Baghdad, including the House of Wisdom. Islam would never recover as a governing system. Over the following centuries, its influence and power waned and all but vanished. Some scholars believe that it is this great insult to Islamic pride that continues to motivate dreams of restoring the caliphate.[3]

In 2014, ISIS leader Abu Bakr al-Baghdadi declared himself the leader of the world's Muslims and ISIS territory in Iraq and Syria its caliphate at the Great Mosque of al-Nuri in Mosul, Iraq, pictured here.

Baghdadi paused at the base of the podium and at each step as he ascended. Muhammad, the prophet and founder of Islam, had reportedly done the same. Before beginning his sermon, Baghdadi cleaned his teeth with a wooden stick, another habit of Muhammad. The entire spectacle was carefully designed to convey a clear image. Baghdadi was the caliph, and he would run things the way that Muhammad had more than a thousand years prior. Even his new name was designed to harken back to the early days of Islam. The original Abu Bakr was the first convert to Islam and the first caliph after Muhammad's death.

The name, the grand ceremony, and the elevation of Baghdadi as the leader of the faithful would have seemed strange to anyone who knew Baghdadi from his earlier life. Baghdadi was born Ibrahim al-Badri in Samarra, Iraq. In his youth he loved to play soccer and study Islam. He loved to lead the neighborhood children in recitations of the Quran. After completing his master's degree in Quranic recitation, he joined the Muslim Brotherhood. Their Salafi ideology was a perfect fit for the young man, but he was unhappy with the Brotherhood's slow approach to world domination. Captured by the Americans after the invasion of Iraq, al-Badri spent ten months teaching the Quran and building a network among the jihadists in the prison where he was held.

After his release, al-Badri began working with al-Qaeda in Iraq as a scholar and judge, handing out harsh penalties for un-Islamic behavior. After he completed his PhD in Quranic sciences, he was elevated to the ruling council of the newly minted Islamic State in Iraq. When the leaders were killed in American airstrikes, Badri took on a new name—and then claimed the throne as the leader of ISIS.[4] As Abu Bakr al-Baghdadi, al-Badri no longer had to content himself with chastising others for failure to adhere to the traditions of the early Muslims. Now he could have anyone who violated his standards killed. With the ascension of ISIS to a caliphate, all of the world's Muslims were supposed to follow his leadership. The death of Osama bin Laden and the weakening status of al-Qaeda allowed Baghdadi to truly come into his own.

HARSH CONDITIONS

As ISIS grew in eastern Syria, Baghdadi finally had the power to enforce Islamic law. Christians had to pay a tax to continue living in ISIS lands. Stonings, beheadings, and dismemberment became common punishments under the violent rule of ISIS. Anyone who opposed the new caliph and his Islamic State was killed, often in grand public spectacles. Tribes who disagreed with the rise of ISIS found themselves targets. Any soldier or government official who would not repent and join the group was also killed. The group expanded in Iraq. The Islamic State now stretched nearly 400 miles (644 kilometers).

Many people in Iraq welcomed ISIS as liberators. The largely Sunni population in western Iraq believed that the mostly Shia government in Baghdad was not their friend. There were rumors, a few confirmed, of atrocities and abuses of Sunnis at the hands of Shia soldiers in the Iraqi Security Forces. ISIS made it perfectly clear who its enemies were. Baghdadi's predecessor had said that Shia, the West, and anyone who worked with them were all enemies of the Islamic State.[5]

In cities like Mosul and Raqqa, ISIS was the sole authority. It ran the government, the schools, and the mosques. Roaming bands of religious police wandered the streets, imposing punishments on anyone who did not meet their standards. Women were beaten for not being covered enough or wearing perfume. Men were attacked if their beards were too short or their pants too long. Children were forced into service with the jihadists or placed into schools that taught and normalized violence in the name of Islam. Christians were required to pay taxes and practice their faith privately. Minority religions like the Yazidis of northern Iraq were rounded up and killed or sold into slavery. The world began to wake to the dangers posed by ISIS, and a military response began in earnest. To preserve its hold on Iraq and Syria, ISIS redoubled its efforts to recruit new fighters from all over the world.

CALLING ALL HOLY WARRIORS

To hold its land against the growing resistance, and to expand its reach, ISIS began recruiting fighters in earnest. The group

An Iraqi fighter from the Peace Brigade waves a flag during fighting with ISIS in Tuz Khurmatu, Iraq, in August 2014. ISIS had only been in official existence for a few months but was already putting up a strong fight against the Iraqi Security Forces and local militias.

JIHAD

The idea of jihad has always been a contentious one in Islam. Many believe that it was only intended to refer to man's struggle to live according to the words of God. Others claim that it is for defensive purposes only. Even Muhammad tried to draw distinctions between a lesser jihad of violent struggle and the greater jihad of daily life. Beginning in the thirteenth century, ideas about jihad began to change. Taqi al-Din Ahmad Ibn Taymiyya thought that jihad should be waged against any leader, even Muslims, who did not rule in accordance with Islam. These ideas were expanded by writers like Sayyid Abu al-A'la Mawdudi, Hasan al-Banna, and Sayyid Qutb. The concept of jihad became far more militant for the followers of these scholars.

Previous assertions against attacking Christians, Jews, and other Muslims were discarded as a radical militant ideology developed around the idea of a global jihad to restore a worldwide caliphate. These writers also expanded the duty to conduct jihad to all Muslims. In wars past, so long as there were other Muslims fighting, it was not required for all Muslims to join the fight.[6] The idea of a militant global jihad is not accepted by most of the world's Muslims. Most Muslims discount the idea entirely or prefer the interpretation that jihad is a personal struggle to live the word of God.

began distributing violent images and videos over social media platforms like Twitter and Facebook. In some cases, the group hijacked popular topics and filled the feeds with gruesome images of executions and torture.[7] ISIS promised recruits endless opportunities to act out their most violent desires, all under the guise of righteous warfare.

The response has been staggering. Between twelve thousand and thirty-one thousand foreign fighters have come from all over the world to join the fight.[8] For many it is a chance for glory or redemption. Others want to belong to something bigger than themselves. Others still are truly angry at the plight of Muslims around the world and see this as their chance to right perceived wrongs. While some have characterized foreign fighters as poor and ignorant, the studies do not support that opinion. In fact, foreign fighters were more likely to come from countries with low inequality, high income, and strong governments. The better predictors were poor assimilation coupled with exposure to and acceptance of jihadist ideology.[9]

ISIS's violent rise to power disturbed the status quo, even for other terrorist organizations. While ISIS made enemies among former friends, its greatest threat was from the enemy abroad. American and coalition efforts to destroy the group were underway. It remains to be seen if drones and Special Operations forces can destroy what ISIS has built in the rough stretches of desert in Syria and Iraq.

5

PRUNING THE

BRANCHES

The relationship between ISIS and al-Qaeda had been shaky from the start. The groups disagreed about who they should fight, how to establish a caliphate, and even what level of violence was appropriate. ISIS was on the rise, and al-Qaeda's power was fading. After Osama bin Laden's death, what little control al-Qaeda had over ISIS weakened even further. It was only natural that the newer group would seek to stretch its wings.

SEPARATION FROM AL-QAEDA

Al-Qaeda in Iraq was founded with $5,000 in seed money from Osama bin Laden himself. Bin Laden's goal had always been the reestablishment of the caliphate. His approach was a slow one, focused on what he called the far enemy, the United States. His intention in giving Zarqawi money to start his own organization was to expand al-Qaeda further and to take control in Iraq, not to create a competitor. The groups' strategies and tactics were too different to be reconciled without some conflict. Al-Qaeda expected Zarqawi to focus on attacking the Americans in Iraq.

Instead, Zarqawi directed much of his violence against Shia Muslims and even other Sunnis. After bin Laden's death, the divide grew even wider.

Ayman al-Zawahiri, an Egyptian doctor and al-Qaeda's second-in-command, was now in charge of the terrorist group. Letters found after bin Laden's death revealed that he thought the establishment of an Islamic State was bound to fail. Its enemies were too strong. If the group lost, it could undo everything for which bin Laden had worked. Zawahiri wrote a letter addressing his group and its affiliates. In it, he warned against fighting Muslim governments. He also told the groups not to attack other Muslims, especially civilians. ISIS, under the leadership of Baghdadi, would ignore the letter and continue its campaign of terror.

Osama bin Laden (*left*) is shown during an interview with a Pakistani journalist in 2001. Earlier that year, bin Laden had planned the September 11 attacks on the United States.

American news magazines *Time* and *Newsweek* announce the death of terrorist leader Osama bin Laden in 2011. Bin Laden was one of the inspirations for the founding of ISIS.

The difference in targets and tactics stems from the differing strategies of the two groups. Daniel Byman, the author of *Al-Qaeda, the Islamic State, and the Global Jihadist Movement*, noted that al-Qaeda wanted to focus on and attack the United States to force it out of the Middle East. Without American forces in the region, Middle East governments would be more vulnerable and could be more easily overthrown by the people in those countries. ISIS would rather attack the local governments directly.[1] This led to several high-profile attacks in Syria, Iraq, Jordan, and now Afghanistan. In most cases, ISIS has focused its efforts against security and intelligence forces in these countries.

In February 2014, these differences finally came to a head. After ISIS refused to accept Zawahiri's directive to stop trying to claim al-Nusra as part of ISIS, al-Qaeda formally cut its ties

DEATH OF THE SHEIK

After the attacks on September 11, 2001, Osama bin Laden was America's primary target. It was thought that he was operating his terror group, al-Qaeda, from the caves of Afghanistan. Little did the American forces know that bin Laden was not in Afghanistan. Bin Laden was hiding in a large compound in Abbottabad in neighboring Pakistan. He was eventually tracked to Pakistan when his courier was witnessed traveling to Abbottabad to deliver messages to bin Laden.

On the night of May 1, 2011, twenty-three Navy SEALS boarded two helicopters headed for the compound. The helicopters had been fitted with devices to quiet the roar of their engines and routers to allow for a stealthy approach. The mission nearly ended in disaster as one of the helicopters crashed on approach inside the compound. Planners had failed to account for the backwash of wind from the propellers against a nearby wall. The SEALS left the crippled chopper and continued their assault.

The doors of the compound were destroyed by C4 explosives. Elite operators poured into the compound, only half sure that bin Laden was inside.[2] The SEALs worked their way through the residential compound, killing a few terrorists who opened fire on them. At the top of the stairs they found their target hiding behind his wives. Eighteen minutes after the ground operation began, Osama bin Laden was dead.[3] Al-Qaeda's number two, Zawahiri, was now in charge, and he was no fan of Zarqawi's rebellious group, which had continued its rampant violence against Muslims under its new leader, Abu Umar al-Baghdadi.

to ISIS. Zawahiri, the leader of al-Qaeda, announced that because ISIS was too violent and continued to target Muslims, it was not part of al-Qaeda. He told the world's Muslims to denounce the group and instead support the Islamic Emirate of Afghanistan, another name for the Taliban.[4] ISIS was on its own.

REJECTION OF ISIS

ISIS's rejection by al-Qaeda was not the first time the group had met resistance. ISIS, in one of its early iterations, had drawn the ire of Sunni tribes in western Iraq. When the Americans initiated the Surge in 2007, tripling the strength of US forces in the country, it found a willing partner. The Sunni tribesmen, known as the Sons of Iraq, became powerful allies in the region and a significant problem for ISIS. With training and equipment from the United States, the Sons of Iraq broke the hold that the jihadists had over several of the western provinces.[5] Sadly, after the United States left, the Iraqi government felt threatened by these Sunni tribes and disbanded the militias.

Meanwhile, the civil war in neighboring Syria provided another fantastic opportunity for ISIS. With the Syrian government busy fighting rebels, other groups sprang up around the country trying to seize control. One such group was al-Nusra. Al-Nusra was founded with the purpose of establishing an Islamic State in the Levant (Syria, Lebanon, Jordan, Palestine/Israel). It had pledged loyalty to al-Qaeda and received a budget for operating expenses from the group. It also seized Syrian oil fields as a source of income. It built up its weapons

A member of the US-backed Syrian Democratic Forces removes an ISIS flag in the town of Tabqa, Syria, in April 2017, while the group headed to Raqqa, Syria, to take on ISIS in its capital.

TRAIN AND EQUIP

It was an admission that stunned the US Senate into silence. The United States had spent $500 million on a program to train and equip moderate Syrian forces that would resist the Syrian government and jihadists. After months of training and equipping these forces, General Lloyd Austin, the commander of US Central Command, the military command responsible for the Middle East and Central Asia, admitted that the existing Syrian force consisted of a mere four or five soldiers. More had been trained, but they either switched sides or simply left their weapons and ran.[6] The 2007 Sons of Iraq program had been such a success that the United States thought it could easily replicate the program in Syria.

The idea is simple enough. Take tribesmen from Syria who want to resist government forces and terrorists, send them for training in Jordan or Turkey, then return them to the battlefield trained and equipped to support the war effort. But the combined threat posed by the Syrian government and the growth of ISIS in the country proved too much to overcome. Without enough people willing to risk their lives to stand up to the regime and the jihadists, it was impossible to build the kind of fighting force that had been created years earlier in Iraq.

stock by raiding groups that had been supplied with weapons by the United States.

To shore up its position in Iraq and draw on the successes of Syrian groups, ISIS claimed that al-Nusra was part of ISIS. The commander of al-Nusra balked at the assertion. Al-Nusra was an al-Qaeda affiliate, not an ISIS offshoot. Zawahiri joined the argument from Afghanistan, telling ISIS to focus on Iraq and leave Syria to al-Nusra and al-Qaeda. ISIS refused to accept the decision and still claims al-Nusra as part of its larger family of terrorist organization. The situation got more complicated in 2016, when al-Nusra rejected both al-Qaeda and ISIS. Al-Nusra renamed itself Conquest of the Levant and renounced any affiliation with the two main terror groups in the region. ISIS's claim of a caliphate was in jeopardy if other Muslim jihadist groups would not pledge their loyalty. A caliph who cannot inspire loyalty from jihadists is hardly a caliph and obviously not in control of a caliphate.

STRIKING THE HEAD

Being the leader of a terrorist group is a bad idea if you want to live a long life. Osama bin Laden was killed in a US raid. Mullah Muhammad Umar, the leader of the Taliban, was repeatedly bombed in his house and cars, though he reportedly survived the attacks only to die of tuberculosis. The founder of al-Qaeda in Iraq, Zarqawi, was killed in a double bombing of a secret meeting he was hosting. His successors al-Masri and Umar al-Baghdadi were both killed in US airstrikes. So far, ISIS's current leader, Abu Bakr al-Baghdadi, has survived, though there are reports of him having been wounded by US airstrikes. Even if he is killed, what would that mean to ISIS? Its has changed leaders several times since the founding of the group.

Taliban supporters burn an American flag during an anti-US protest on the first anniversary of Osama bin Laden's death in Pakistan in 2012. Even years after his death, bin Laden still remains a powerful figure in jihadist circles, inspiring new generations of terrorists to take on the West.

One theory behind the resilience of the group is that its leaders have all been figureheads. The real leadership is behind the scenes and made up of former Iraqi army officers loyal to Saddam Hussein.[7] When the United States invaded Iraq in 2003, it quickly set up an office to manage the reestablishment of government in Iraq. Paul Bremmer, the leader of the effort, known as the head of the Coalition Provisional Authority of Iraq, decided to disband the Iraqi army and throw anyone who had been in Saddam's political party (the Baath party) out of the government. Now there were millions of unemployed—and armed—Iraqis unhappy with the Americans. It was almost incvitable that this would lead to the country falling into chaos and creating an environment that would allow for the creation of a group like ISIS.

Perhaps Baghdadi's death would be different. No one has claimed the caliphate since the 1920s. His death could disrupt ISIS because there is no one else as qualified to be caliph. But as long as ISIS maintains its caliphate, it will continue to be a threat that spreads its poison around the world. While the group is losing ground in Syria and Iraq, it continues to grow in other places, like Nigeria, Libya, and Indonesia, where it has inspired numerous followers to start their own terror organizations.

6

DISTANT

SEEDLINGS

To establish a global caliphate, ISIS must expand its territory beyond the small swathes of land it controls in the Middle East. ISIS put out the call for all the world's Muslims to come and fight jihad in Iraq and Syria, but some supporters and affiliated groups have preferred to stay closer to home. Groups in Nigeria, Libya, Indonesia, and Afghanistan have all pledged loyalty to ISIS. They represent the dangerous potential for ISIS to inspire others to violence against those around them.

BOKO HARAM

As much as ISIS or al-Qaeda might like to claim the title, the most violent terrorist group in the world is Boko Haram in Nigeria, Africa. In 2014, ISIS killed 6,073 people. Boko Haram killed 6,644.[1] Fortunately for ISIS, Boko Haram has pledged its loyalty to the group and begun calling itself the Islamic State in West Africa. In Boko Haram, ISIS has found a kindred spirit with which to expand the Islamic State's reach across the globe. The name Boko Haram is a mixture of the local language

Women in Nigeria protest the taking of hundreds of young schoolgirls by the terrorist group Boko Haram in 2014. Although it doesn't share all the same ideals as ISIS, Boko Haram is considered an affiliate of the Islamic State.

and Arabic. *Boko* means "fake" in Hausa, an African language. *Haram* means "forbidden" in Arabic. The two words together are used to refer to Western education as fake and forbidden. The name refers to the colonial period when Britain set up secular and Christian schools throughout Nigeria.[2]

A bird's-eye view of Nigeria looks almost like two different countries. In the south, along the ocean, there are massive cities with perhaps the highest population density in the world. Offshore oilrigs pump money into the economy here. There is a government, and public services are available to the people. The area is nearly entirely Christian. In northwest Nigeria, things are very different. Poor farmers strive to eke out a living from the near-desert soil around them. There are almost no government services here. Nearly all the citizens are Muslim. It is from this northwest corner of Nigeria that a new terror threat arose.

In 2002, Mohammad Yusuf started a school in this desolate area to teach children about Islam. He believed in a Salafi, jihadist version of Islam where everyone should live like Muhammad and the early Muslims and fight for their faith. Over the next decade, his group would be a violent force for evil in the country. It carried out attacks against police and military targets and even a United Nations headquarters. The group began looking for foreigners to kidnap for ransom. The group frequently worked with al-Qaeda jihadists in the region. Boko Haram had seized several towns in northwest Nigeria, enforcing its own harsh brand of Islamic law. In 2015,

Nigerian mothers whose daughters were kidnapped by Boko Haram in 2014 are seen crying during a rally against the terrorist organization in 2016.

BRING BACK OUR GIRLS

In April 2014, Boko Haram caught the world's attention when members kidnapped 276 girls from a school in Chibok, Nigeria. The leader of Boko Haram announced that the girls would be sold as slaves. The girls were locked up, and many were forced to serve as wives to Boko Haram fighters.[3] A social media campaign known by the hashtag #BringBackOurGirls began trending around the world. Even First Lady Michelle Obama took a picture of herself holding a card bearing the slogan.[4] The Nigerian government has repeatedly promised to free the girls but has not been successful.

Some of the girls have escaped the group, and 82 were released in a deal between Boko Haram and the Nigerian government in 2017. Those who have gotten away from Boko Haram tell tales of living in constant fear while held by their captors. The girls are forced into sexual relations with jihadists, often bearing them children. Sadly, those with children who escape find problems back at home. Because they have children from their rapes by jihadists, they are not welcome in many social circles back home. Caught between the brutal fighters and their suspicious neighbors, these girls face incredible hardships brought on by their kidnapping at the hands of a terror group loyal to ISIS.

MOTHER OF ALL BOMBS

A short distance from the location where ISIS had killed two men was a network of impenetrable caves that served as an ISIS headquarters. Sending in soldiers, even highly trained Special Operations forces, would have been extremely dangerous because of the terrain and the defensive options it gave the entrenched terrorists. With the internal structure of the caves unknown bunker-buster missiles were difficult to target. Surface bombs and missiles would not reach the forces underground. Fortunately, the United States had developed a weapon that was just what the situation needed.

The GBU-43/B is named Massive Ordinance Air Blast (MOAB), but no one calls it that. For most, MOAB stands for "Mother of All Bombs." It is a nearly 22,000-pound bomb that explodes with the force of eleven tons of TNT. It is the largest non-nuclear bomb in the world.[5] On April 13, 2017, a C-130 military transport plane flew over the network of caves in Afghanistan and dropped a large sled out of the back. On the sled was the MOAB. The news of the use of the bomb and a video of the explosion quickly went viral.

When the dust settled, nearly a hundred suspected ISIS terrorists were dead. Those not caught in the blast may have thought themselves safe below ground in the tunnels. They were wrong. The MOAB explodes with such force that its shockwaves alone can be lethal. Additionally, the fireball generated by the explosion sucks all the oxygen from the surrounding air. Terrorists deep in the tunnels would have asphyxiated as the oxygen was sucked from the air they were breathing.

the group pledged loyalty to ISIS. ISIS accepted the group and encouraged Muslims who could not make it to Syria and Iraq to join up with its partner in Nigeria. But Boko Haram, like its parent in Iraq and Syria, was losing ground fast. It lost the few towns it had to government forces and has been relegated to the wilds of the northwest. But it continues to strike from the shadows. Boko Haram has begun carrying out attacks in neighboring countries. Some of its fighters have left for nearby Libya to contribute to the fight there.[6]

DRIVING A WEDGE

Terrorist groups like ISIS and al-Qaeda thrive in spaces where the government is weak or nonexistent. Since the fall of dictator Muamar al-Qaddafi, Libya has presented an excellent opportunity for the group to gain a foothold and expand the Islamic State. The trouble started during the Arab Spring. Rebels in eastern Libya overwhelmed Libyan security forces and claimed independence from Libya. Most of Libya's natural resources, including its valuable oil wells, are in the east. As Qaddafi gathered his troops and began to march east, the world responded. The United Nations authorized an attack on the army because of the humanitarian threat it posed.

The attack left more than Qaddafi's military in shambles. Unable to maintain power, Qaddafi's regime collapsed. He was captured by rebels and killed in the street. Libya was free of a brutal dictator who had reigned for fifty years. It should have been a happy time, but the country descended into chaos. Former government factions and military forces began facing off from opposite sides of the country. The many tribes of Libya entered the fray on both sides, further complicating the fight. The world had no plan for what to do after it toppled Qaddafi.

The fall of Qaddafi and the subsequent chaos was a perfect opportunity for ISIS. It seized the eastern city of Derna, Libya, and began to institute Islamic law. Video clips began to find their way onto the internet, and they showed ISIS carrying out shootings, beheadings, stonings, and even crucifixions.[7] Derna is in the heart of the most oil-rich region of Libya. It was an incredible source of income for ISIS. But its hold on Derna didn't last long, and it was driven out of the town by an unlikely enemy. Forces loyal to al-Qaeda attacked the ISIS forces in Derna and drove them from the city.

Driven from the rich natural resources in the east and unwelcome in the largely secular west, ISIS set up shop in the center of the country in an area called Sirte. Fortunately for ISIS, the Libyan forces in the east and west are focused on each other and not the growing threat in the center of the country. American bombers targeted ISIS in Sirte, killing eighty supposed fighters in a strike in January 2017, but the group simply moved south.[8] The countries surrounding Libya have all closed their borders, with Tunisia going so far as to create a giant wall of dirt between the two countries. But ISIS has continued to grow, even in its paltry territory in the wilds of Libya. As rival factions continue to attack each other in the east and west, ISIS watches and waits for its chance to rise again and expand the Islamic State in Libya.

A man walks across the rubble left behind after the United States dropped the Mother of All Bombs (MOAB), the most powerful non-nuclear bomb, on ISIS targets in Afghanistan in 2017.

EASTWARD EXPANSION

Afghanistan has been the domain of al-Qaeda since its fierce battles with the Soviets in the 1980s. Recently a new kind of jihadist is rising and active in the country. The chickens that al-Qaeda released in Iraq and Syria have come home to roost. Poor governance and security in Afghanistan have created an environment where the group can flourish in the seams. In March 2017, ISIS operatives executed two men accused of being spies. A few days later, the group, disguised as doctors, attacked a hospital, killing thirty-eight people.[9]

The Taliban and al-Qaeda have not taken kindly to the intrusion on their lands. The Taliban have formed special forces units specifically tasked with attacking ISIS.[10] Afghanistan has long been known as the Graveyard of Empires. The British failed to achieve success there, and the colonial empire was soon in decline. The Soviet Union spent ten years sending its sons to die in the harsh mountains. Within three years of leaving Afghanistan, the Soviet Union collapsed. America has so far survived thirteen years in the country with few ill effects.

ISIS is the latest empire to challenge the tribes of Afghanistan in the ultimate battle for control of the caliphate. It is ironic that no matter who wins, the Muslims of the world will not pledge allegiance to either group. Unfortunately, there is no shortage of unstable individuals around the world who will pledge loyalty. In the next chapter, we will look at how ISIS is expanding its influence even as its physical territory shrinks.

SPREADING

CANOPY

In addition to spawning like-minded terror groups, ISIS has been working to increase its influence on the world. From assisting or claiming lone wolf attacks, to creating threats against tourism, ISIS has exploited any chance to sow terror around the world. These attacks, and the threat of more, are reason for concern as the United States and its coalition partners attempt to smother ISIS in its crib. Defeating the group in Iraq and Syria is important, but the group may continue to pose a threat from the internet.

LONE WOLVES

While ISIS has encouraged every Muslim in the world to make the journey to Syria and Iraq to fight with the caliphate, many cannot get there. Some are turned away at the borders. Others are apprehended as they try to make arrangements for their journey. Shortly after the announcement of the caliphate, Abu Muhammad al-Adnani, an ISIS spokesman, called for attacks abroad. He advised any Muslim who wanted to help the cause

HAKIM KETUA

A suspected terrorist arrives in court in Jakarta, Indonesia, to stand trial for a planned bombing in support of an Indonesian terrorist group that is closely affilliated with ISIS.

to attack Christians and Jews in their own countries. Abu Bakr al-Baghdadi, the leader of ISIS, has also called on followers to "erupt volcanoes of jihad everywhere."[1] These are not hollow threats. Across the globe, individuals have pledged allegiance to ISIS and carried out attacks on its behalf.

Lone wolf attacks are so dangerous because they are hard to predict and even harder to stop. Any individual with access to weapons who is inspired by ISIS's message of violence can carry out attacks on the group's behalf. Adnani, ISIS's spokesman, suggested a variety of attack methods, from poison, to rocks, to barehanded strangulation, to crashing a truck into crowds of people.[2] Zealots across the planet have taken Adnani's words to heart. There have been a few cases of lone wolves ramming trucks into crowds.

Germany is well known for its Christmas markets. Entire city squares are turned into festive spaces devoted to the holiday season. The squares are packed with revelers and shoppers who are eager to find a unique gift or just enjoy the communal buzz of the markets. Monday, December 19, 2016, was like any other night at the Berlin market. Hundreds of people milled about enjoying glasses of mulled wine. In the distance, a truck approached. Rather than slowing down as it approached the colorful tents, the truck accelerated. It plowed through the festive stalls, mowing down dozens of shoppers. The attack left twelve dead and forty-eight injured. A few months later, a similar attack in Stockholm killed four and wounded fifteen.

The drivers in both attacks had pledged loyalty to ISIS, and the group quickly claimed credit for the attacks against the West. The horrific attacks, carried out with the simplest of weapons, demonstrate the danger that these lone wolves pose to the enemies of ISIS.

ISIS IN THE FAR EAST

While ISIS is usually thought of as a Middle Eastern organization that focuses on Western governments, the group has not limited its gaze to the West. ISIS groups have sprung up in the Philippines, Afghanistan, Pakistan, and Indonesia. While some of the groups have explicitly targeted people with white skin, other groups have attacked Muslim gatherings with bombs and guns.

Cesare Tavella, an Italian citizen, was jogging home after swimming at the American International School in Bangladesh. He was jogging through the diplomatic zone. The diplomatic zone had always been a safe space. ISIS was about to demonstrate that no place was safe. Two gunmen ambushed Tavella. They fired three shots, killing the Italian. The gunmen jumped onto a motorcycle and fled the scene. ISIS quickly claimed responsibility. They issued a message that said, "We say to all citizens of the Crusader coalition, you will not be safe in the Muslim lands, and this is just the beginning."[3]

In the Philippines there have been multiple incidents where professors and other secular and religious figures have been attacked in their homes. The attacks are usually carried out with machetes, to gruesome effect. ISIS has claimed the attacks as part of its campaign. The attacks show that while the primary target might be Western governments, no place is out of reach for the group, despite its remote location in the deserts of Iraq and Syria.

ONGOING THREATS

To manage its terrorist network, ISIS has declared several regions outside of Iraq and Syria as *wilayats*, or provinces. These wilayats exist in Algeria, Libya, Yemen, Saudi Arabia, and Egypt. The idea for these provinces of the Islamic State is as old as the idea of a caliphate. Throughout the Islamic conquests in the seventh and eighth centuries CE, conquerors would establish a local governor, or *wali*, responsible for managing the province and collecting and relaying taxes back to the seat of the caliph. Wilayats of old were the source of periodic upheaval as foreign governors tried to impose the will of a distant caliphate on the citizens of the provinces. The modern versions are pale imitations of their prede-

cessors. These wilayats control no real land and no seat of authority from which to impose their position. The modern wilayats thrive in ungoverned spaces like the Sinai Peninsula in Egypt. But their tenuous grasp on these regions does not make them any less dangerous.

In Egypt, the response to ISIS has been swift and violent. The Egyptian military is not usually allowed to operate in the Sinai because of a treaty agreement with Israel. In this case, Israel gave its permission. Egyptian tanks rolled across the peninsula

In August 2016, ISIS claimed responsibility for a car bombing outside a military recruitment center in Aden, Yemen. Although primarily in Iraq and Syria, ISIS has been able to spread its message of terror far and wide.

for the first time since 1972. Tanks surrounded the northwestern villages, formerly havens for ISIS fighters, as soldiers began to clear terrorists from the villages. As usual, ISIS has melted into the desert and continues to plan its efforts against the Egyptian government and the massive tourist industry in Egypt.

Other ISIS wilayats are in less governed spaces. Yemen and Libya are in such a state of chaos that the group can operate freely there. These areas are not without danger for ISIS, as

DOWN IN FLAMES

Sharm al-Sheik is one of the most beautiful beaches in the world. This resort town, located on the tip of the Sinai Peninsula, is renowned for its snorkeling and its thriving tourist resorts. On October 31, 2015, a Russian plane lifted off from the tiny airport with 224 people on board. Most of the passengers were tourists returning from their beach vacations to face the harsh Russian winter ahead. They never made it home. Twenty minutes after takeoff, the plane disintegrated in the skies above the Sinai Peninsula. There were no survivors. It was the worst air disaster ever for Russia. When ISIS claimed credit, it became its most successful strike in its short history.

As the investigation dragged on, the cause was unclear. Some claimed a maintenance issue. Others thought a missile brought the plane down. The flight data recorder was found and the tape was consistent with an explosion. The next issue of *Dabiq*, ISIS's online magazine, featured a soda can that the group claimed was used as a bomb to bring the plane down. A maintenance worker had snuck the can on board.[4] Police at the airport were either complicit or incompetent for the bomb to have been smuggled onto the plane. The saddest picture to come from the coverage is a child's single ragged pink shoe amid the wreckage of the plane.

both are embroiled in civil wars between the tribes who would see ISIS as another target. Saudi Arabia and Algeria are more firmly governed but still find themselves challenged to find the terrorists and root them out. The spread of ISIS has countered some of its losses on the ground as a new wilayat rose up in Afghanistan recently to challenge the Taliban and al-Qaeda.

A WORLD IN SHADE

Since the declaration of the caliphate in 2014, ISIS has carried out or inspired 140 attacks in nearly thirty countries. More than two thousand people have been killed. Thousands more have been injured.[5] Refugees from the conflicts in Iraq and Syria have flooded Europe. ISIS attacks have created distrust among the citizens of Europe and created difficulties for refugees seeking a better life. One of the core tenets of ISIS is that the Western world is at war with Muslims. By attacking while posing as refugees, the group hopes to convince refugees that there is no hope for them but ISIS. ISIS claims that once it controls the world, all Muslims will live in peace and prosperity. But the examples of Mosul and Raqqa show that the group is only interested in furthering its own objectives through violent means.

Uncertainty created by ISIS attacks has wreaked havoc on the tourism industry around the world. Countries like Egypt rely heavily on tourism. More than three million Russians used to visit the country each year.[6] Hotels that used to generate $250 million each month in income stand empty. Attacks on civilians are designed to drive away tourists and destabilize governments because of the loss of revenue. Attacks in Tunisia and France have hurt the tourism industry in those countries as well. Tourism in Europe is at its lowest level since the 1970s.[7]

By expanding its base and inspiring like-minded individuals, ISIS has been able to exert influence far beyond its remote

A family walks through the Chamakor refugee camp outside Mosul, Iraq. Because of fighting with ISIS, thousands of Iraqis and Syrians have been forced out of their homes and into numerous refugee camps across the Middle East.

corners of Iraq and Syria. While the group is losing ground quickly to local and international forces, its reach seems to be expanding. Unchecked, the group threatens to throw the world into a dark place dominated by a religious group who seeks to enforce a barbaric code of medieval laws. ISIS's rise to power will not go unchallenged. While military forces can destroy the physical presence of the group, it will take a global effort led by Muslims to root out the vicious ideology that motivates the group and its followers. In the next chapter we'll look at the likely defeat of the caliphate and how it might evolve to survive the loss of its lands.

FELLING THE

BEHEMOTH

The days of ISIS are numbered. A global coalition of military forces is driving the group from its strongholds in Iraq and Syria. Muslims throughout the world have rejected the group's claim on the Islamic faith. Even the terror groups from which ISIS evolved have denounced the group for its gruesome violence and indiscriminate attacks. As the group loses ground, it will evolve to try to maintain its claim to be the caliphate. The world will have to address the new threat posed by the ideology that motivated the group and the conditions that allowed it to flourish.

LOSING GROUND

Local military forces have been critical in the fight against the violent rise of ISIS. In 2007, it was local forces, armed and trained by the United States, that nearly destroyed the predecessor to ISIS in Iraq. If not for poor governance after the United States' withdrawal, the group might not have ever

United States secretary of defense James Mattis (*left*) is seen attending a NATO summit meeting in 2017. Along with President Donald Trump, Mattis was there to discuss NATO playing a bigger role in the fight against ISIS.

recovered. After the seizure of Mosul in 2014, ISIS controlled a large section of desert from Raqqa, Syria, to central Iraq. Since 2016, ISIS has been losing ground on every front. The group is facing the loss of the lands that give it some legitimacy as a state and a caliphate. Even its remote provinces are under attack and losing ground.

The loss of ground has made the group more dangerous, as it is facing extinction. The group finds itself in a position of vulnerability, and its only option is to fight for its life. Sun Tzu's *The Art of War* notes that an enemy on death's door is the most dangerous because, "If they will face death, there is nothing they may not achieve. Officers and men alike will put forth their uttermost strength."[1] As ISIS loses ground, it is lashing out in new and innovative ways, including the use of drone warfare and crude chemical weapons.

Mosul had been a source of shame for the Iraqi government. Some thirty thousand Iraqi soldiers and another thirty thousand police fled the city when it was attacked by fifteen hundred ISIS militants in 2014. Mosul was a significant prize for ISIS. It captured a number of American tanks and armored vehicles, including several helicopters.[2] After months of planning, the Iraqi army struck back. In January 2017, Iraqi Security Forces drove ISIS from the eastern half of the city. They surrounded the militants in an area across the Tigris River. The city's residents are free of ISIS rule, but there is much to be done to restore the town to its pre-war state.[3]

ISIS's stronghold in Raqqa, Syria, is also facing threats. Syrian Defense Forces are starting their approach on the city, clearing smaller towns along the way. Turkish forces are advancing from the north, and Kurdish forces are contributing to the fight from the northeast and northwest. As the forces close in from every side, ISIS is facing strangulation in the desert of Syria. The violent rise of ISIS has crested, and the group may be heading toward extinction.

THE COMING CRASH

Defeating ISIS on the ground will not eliminate the threat from the group. There has never been a purely military solution to the problem of terrorism and extremism. Bombs and guns may kill terrorists, but the friends and families of those terrorists may be inspired to violence because of the loss of their loved ones. Since the beginning of the Global War on Terrorism in 2001, the number of deaths blamed on terrorists increased by nearly 900 percent. Terrorists were responsible for a record number of deaths in 2014, the deadliest year on record when it comes to deaths caused by terrorism.[4]

That ISIS has lost control of Mosul and is losing ground everywhere suggests that the military is an important part of any solution. ISIS must control land somewhere to have any hope of continuing to claim that it is an Islamic State and a caliphate for all the world's Muslims. A state with no land and a caliphate that physically controls no people is hardly a force that could ever dominate the world. Yet this is the future that ISIS is facing. Osama bin Laden had warned against forcing the establishment of a caliphate for

this very reason, saying in a recently discovered letter, "[I]t will fail."[5] Its failure would doom the project and forfeit any future efforts at establishing a physical Islamic State.

An Iraqi Emergency Response Division soldier carries a rocket-propelled grenade toward the villages west of Mosul, which were still being held by ISIS in February 2017.

DANGEROUS INNOVATION

It was a relatively new site on the battlefield. In October 2016, Kurdish forces in Iraq and their French advisors heard the tell-tale high whine of a toy drone above them. The drones could be fitted with cameras and used for surveillance. The Kurdish soldiers shot the drone out of the sky. When they went to inspect the device, they noticed something strange. Something was attached to the drone. When they leaned in to inspect the drone, it exploded, killing two Kurdish soldiers and wounding two French advisors.[6] It was the first known use of a toy drone as a weapon in war. Since that first attack, ISIS has gotten more sophisticated. Drones are now fitted with triggers that allow ISIS to drop bombs remotely instead of crashing the devices into enemy forces.

Any innovation triggers more innovation. As America scrambled to address the new threat, a variety of anti-drone weapons have made the rounds. Some seek to disrupt the signal controlling the drone. Other devices fire a net to trap the drone. Cruder weapons simply shoot the drone out of the sky. Some airports are training falcons and eagles to snatch the drones out of the sky. The Defense Advance Projects Research Agency, or DARPA, known for developing high-tech solutions to problems on the battlefield, is developing a laser to destroy enemy drones. The lasers can be carried or mounted on vehicles—even on American drones—to blast enemy drones out of the sky in a real-life scene straight out of a video game.[7]

ISIS will retreat to the internet as it loses its lands in Iraq and Syria. Without a home base, the wilayats around the world will also fall. From the internet, ISIS will continue to try to inspire violence and plan attacks with the goal of reestablishing the physical caliphate. J. M. Berger, an ISIS scholar, noted that while the printing press allowed for the spread of information,and the telephone allowed for instant communication, social media combines both, "incredibly multiplying the effect of radical messaging."[8] Social media giants are already working to combat the group in cyberspace.

A LASTING SOLUTION

If the military cannot defeat ISIS by itself, how can the group ever be eliminated? It will require a combined effort from many areas of society. Muslims across the globe have denounced ISIS and rightfully claim the group does not represent Islam. These voices must be given more attention. Muslim scholars are best poised to address the level to which Islamic scripture justifies violence. Communities must do more to engage with each other and understand when propagandists and recruiters are operating amid their children. The version of Islam that ISIS claims must be differentiated from the true nature of the religion and its mostly peaceful adherents.

Failure to assimilate and poor governance have been listed as factors for ISIS recruitment in the West and in Middle Eastern countries. Second- and third-generation children of immigrants to Western countries are over-represented in surveys of foreign fighters. The West must do a better job of fostering inclusive societies that look beyond race and culture. This means improving social programs and eliminating discrimination in the workplace and schools. Providing programs that encourage communication about these issues within communities may help heal some of the divides.

Women from the Kurdish Peshmerga are seen undergoing training at a YPG camp in Erbil, Iraq. The Peshmerga, who are from the independent region of Iraqi Kurdistan, have been on the front lines of the fight against ISIS since the group emerged in 2014.

SOCIAL MEDIA WAR

In September 2014, social media giant Twitter had had enough. ISIS was using the platform to distribute propaganda and gruesome images of violence. Over the next few months, Twitter suspended tens of thousands of accounts.[9] Some estimates put the number of banned accounts at more than 100,000. But there's a very tricky thin line between blocking free speech and defeating hate speech. ISIS has many accounts that create content. A larger number of accounts spread the terrorist group's tweets. An even larger number of accounts follow these propagandists as consumers of the content. While it is easy to argue for banning creators of violent content, how far should the purge go? Retweeters are spreading the violent messages and subject to banning, but what about those who follow and do not retweet? Exposure to jihadist propaganda is a common element in many who fight for the group or commit violence at home. Not every person who views violent content will be inspired to commit violence, but should they be subjected to increased scrutiny? Such efforts are likely to focus on Muslims and be labeled as racist. It's a slippery slope with no easy fix.

As long as there is instability in the Middle East, there will be danger from violent extremist organizations. They exploit the anger of the citizens of these countries and thrive in the ungoverned or poorly governed spaces. These governments and their militaries must be more inclusive and protect all of the citizens' rights and not just a privileged few based on tribal or religious affiliation. Economic aid to strengthen economies and provide opportunities for the development of strong government institutions that prioritize human rights and dignity will help stabilize the region. A stable Middle East and an inclusive West will do much to prevent the rise of another group like ISIS.

ISIS is no longer rising. From its bloody beginnings to its desperate attempts to maintain relevance, the group has been a force for evil in the world. Its use of violence against those with whom it disagrees has no place in the modern world. The world has rejected ISIS. Its own faith has rejected it. As it retreats to its dark corners of the internet, the world must not ignore the conditions that allowed for the violent rise of ISIS. It is the only way to prevent the return of the group or another like it.

CHAPTER NOTES

Chapter 1: Roots of Evil

1. Abdullah Azzam, "The Defence of Muslim Lands, The First Obligation After Faith," accessed May 26, 2017, http://www.religioscope.com/info/doc/jihad/azzam_defence_3_chap1.htm.
2. David Commins, *The Wahhabi Mission and Saudi Arabia* (London: I.B.Tauris & Co Ltd., 2006), p. 174.
3. Michel Chossudovsky, "The Spoils of War: Afghanistan's Multibillion Dollar Heroin Trade," Global Research, May 2005, http://www.globalresearch.ca/the-spoils-of-war-afghanistan-s-multibillion-dollar-heroin-trade/91.
4. Ibid.
5. Chossudovsky, "Spoils of War," figures updated in 2017.
6. Mark N. Katz, "Lessons of the Soviet Withdrawal from Afghanistan," Middle East Policy Council, accessed May 26, 2017, http://www.mepc.org/articles-commentary/commentary/lessons-soviet-withdrawal-afghanistan.
7. Norimitsu Onishi, "A Tale of the Mullah and Muhammad's Amazing Cloak," *New York Times* (online), December 19, 2001, http://www.nytimes.com/2001/12/19/international/asia/a-tale-of-the-mullah-and-muhammads-amazing-cloak.html.
8. "Afghanistan Wakes after Night of Continuous Bombing," CNN.com, October 7, 2001, http://www.cnn.com/2001/US/10/07/gen .america.under.attack/

Chapter 2: Branching Out

1. Mary Anne Weaver, "The Short, Violent Life of Abu Musab al-Zarqawi," *Atlantic* (online), July 2006, https://www.theatlantic.com/magazine/archive/2006/07/the-short-violent-life-of-abu-musab-al-zarqawi/304983/.
2. James M. Breslow, "Who Was the Founder of ISIS," PBS.org, May 17, 2016, http://www.pbs.org/wgbh/frontline/article/who-was-the-founder-of-isis/.

3. Michako Kakutani, "Review: Black Flags, Tracing the Birth of ISIS," *New York Times* (online), November 30, 2105, https://www.nytimes.com/2015/12/01/books/review-black-flags-tracing-the-birth-of-isis.html?_r=0.

4. Ron Kampeas, "Laurence Foley," *Washington Post* (online), October 29, 2002, https://www.washingtonpost.com/archive/local/2002/10/29/laurence-foley/1eadea21-3a8b-496a-ba14-f5f8912f676c/?utm_term=.475a6f11e6c8.

5. Weaver, "The Short, Violent Life of Abu Musab al-Zarqawi."

6. Jamie McIntyre, Barbara Starr, Henry Schuster, and Randa Habib, "Painstaking Operation Led to Zarqawi," CNN.com, June 8, 2006, http://www.cnn.com/2006/WORLD/meast/06/08/iraq.al.zarqawi.1929/.

7. Ellen Knickmeyer, "Blood on Our Hands," Foreign Policy (online), February 21, 2011, https://foreignpolicy.com/articles/2010/10/25/Blood_on_Our_Hands?page=full.

Chapter 3: **Spring Growth**

1. David Petraeus, "How We Won in Iraq," Foreign Policy (online), October 29, 2013, http://foreignpolicy.com/2013/10/29/how-we-won-in-iraq/.

2. Mark Landler, "The Afghan War and the Evolution of Obama," *New York Times* (online), January 1, 2017, https://www.nytimes.com/2017/01/01/world/asia/obama-afghanistan-war.html?_r=0.

3. Petraeus, "How We Won in Iraq."

4. William McCants, "The Believer," Brooking Institute, September 1, 2015, http://csweb.brookings.edu/content/research/essays/2015/thebeliever.html.

5. David Ignatius, "How ISIS Spread in the Middle East," *Atlantic* (online), October 29, 2015, https://www.theatlantic.com/international/archive/2015/10/how-isis-started-syria-iraq/412042/.

6. Amanda Bennett, "Daesh? ISIS? Islamic State? Why What We Call the Paris Attackers Matters," *Washington Post* (online), November 25, 2015, https://www.washingtonpost.com/news/in-theory/wp/2015/11/25/daesh-isis-islamic-state-why-what-we-call-the-paris-attackers-matters/?utm_term=.b698fed5b7ae.

Chapter 4: **Rotten Fruit**

1. William McCants, "How ISIS Got Its Flag," *Atlantic* (online), September 22, 2015, https://www.theatlantic.com/international/ archive/2015/09/isis-flag-apocalypse/406498/.

2. Vartan Gregorian, *Islam: A Mosaic, Not a Monolith* (Washington, DC: Brookings Institution Press, 2003), pp. 26–38.

3. Bernard Lewis, "The Roots of Muslim Rage," *Atlantic* (online), September 1990, https://www.theatlantic.com/magazine/ archive/1990/09/the-roots-of-muslim-rage/304643/.

4. William McCants, "The Believer," Brookings Institute (online), September 1, 2015, http://csweb.brookings.edu/content/research/ essays/2015/thebeliever.html.

5. Abu Omar al-Baghdadi's 12th Speech, Audio Recording, September 24, 2008.

6. Michael G. Knapp, "The Concept and Practice of Jihad in Islam," *Parameters*, Spring 2003, http://ssi.armywarcollege.edu/pubs/ parameters/articles/03spring/knapp.pdf.

7. Warwick Ashford, "Jihadists in Iraq Hijack World Cup Hashtags," *Computer Weekly* (online), June 23, 2014, http://www.computerweekly .com/news/2240223131/Jihadists-in-Iraq-hijack-World-Cup-hashtags.

8. Richard Barret on *PBS Newshour*, "The Number of Foreign Recruits to the Islamic State Is Booming, But Not in the U.S." PBS.org, December 8, 2015, http://www.pbs.org/newshour/bb/the-number-of-foreign- recruits-to-the-islamic-state-is-booming-but-not-in-the-u-s/.

9. Ephraim Benmelech and Esteban F. Klor, "What Explains the Flow of Foreign Fighters to ISIS?" Kellogg School of Management, Northwestern University, April 2016, http://www.kellogg.northwestern .edu/faculty/benmelech/html/BenmelechPapers/ISIS_April_13_ 2016_Effi_final.pdf.

Chapter 5: **Pruning the Branches**

1. Daniel Byman, "Comparing Al Qaeda and ISIS: Different Goals, Different Targets," Brookings Institute, April 29, 2015, https://www .brookings.edu/testimonies/comparing-al-qaeda-and-isis-different-goals- different-targets/.

2. Jonathan Mahler, "What Do We Really Know About Osama bin Laden's Death," *New York Times* (online), October 15, 2015, https://www.nytimes.com/2015/10/18/magazine/what-do-we-really-know-about-osama-bin-ladens-death.html?_r=0.

3. Nicholas Schmidle, "Getting Bin Laden," *New Yorker* (online), August 8, 2011, http://www.newyorker.com/magazine/2011/08/08/getting-bin-laden.

4. Jack Moore, "Al-Qaeda's Zawahiri Calls on Supporters to Reject ISIS and Support Taliban," *Newsweek* (online), August 22, 2016, http://www.newsweek.com/al-qaedas-zawahiri-calls-supporters-reject-isis-and-support-taliban-492337.

5. Mark Wilbanks and Efraim Karsh, "How the 'Sons of Iraq' Stabilized Iraq," *Middle East Quarterly* 17, no. 4 (2010), pp. 57–70.

6. David A. Graham, "Only '4 or 5' US Trained Soldiers Remain in Fight against ISIS," *Atlantic* (online), September 16, 2015, https://www.theatlantic.com/notes/2015/09/only-4-or-5-us-trained-fighters-remain-in-fight-against-isis/405640/.

7. Naina Bajekel, "Why ISIS Can Survive Without Baghdadi," *Time* (online), November 14, 2014, http://time.com/3585629/isis-isil-baghdadi-survive/.

Chapter 6: Distant Seedlings

1. Edward Delman, "The World's Deadliest Terrorist Organization," *Atlantic* (online), November 18, 2015, https://www.theatlantic.com/international/archive/2015/11/isis-boko-haram-terrorism/416673/.

2. "Exactly What Does the Phrase Boko Haram Mean," BBC.com, May 13, 2014, http://www.bbc.com/news/blogs-magazine-monitor-27390954.

3. "Beyond Chibok," UNICEF, 2015, https://www.unicef.org/infobycountry/files/Beyond_Chibok.pdf.

4. Michelle Obama, Twitter, May 7, 2104, https://twitter.com/flotus44/status/464148654354628608.

5. "GBU-43/B 'Mother of All Bombs," Global Security.org, April 13, 2017, http://www.globalsecurity.org/military/systems/munitions/moab.htm.

6. "Boko Haram," Mapping Militant Organizations, Stanford University, August 26, 2016, http://web.stanford.edu/group/mappingmilitants/cgi-bin/groups/view/553?highlight=boko+haram.

7. John Lee Anderson, "ISIS Rises in Libya," *New Yorker* (online), August 4, 2015, http://www.newyorker.com/news/news-desk/isis-rises-in-libya.

8. Eric Schmitt, "Warnings of a Powder Keg in Libya as ISIS Regroups," *New York Times* (online), March 21, 2017, https://www.nytimes.com/2017/03/21/world/africa/libya-isis.html.

9. Mirren Gidda, "Why ISIS Is Failing to Build a Caliphate in Afghanistan," *Newsweek*, March 25, 2017, http://www.newsweek.com/afghanistan-isis-taliban-caliphate-kabul-bombing-574198.

10. Dawood Azami, "Why Taliban Special Forces Are Fighting the Islamic State," BBC.com, December 18, 2015, http://www.bbc.com/news/world-asia-35123748.

Chapter 7: Spreading Canopy

1. Jessica Lewis McFate, Harleen Gambhir, and Evan Sterling, "ISIS's Global Messaging Strategy Fact Sheet," Institute for the Study of War, December 2014, http://understandingwar.org/sites/default/files/GLOBAL%20ROLLUP%20Update.pdf.

2. Robin Wright, "After the Islamic State," *New Yorker* (online), December 12, 2016, http://www.newyorker.com/magazine/2016/12/12/after-the-islamic-state.

3. Sugam Pokharel and Holly Yan, "ISIS Says It Killed an Italian on the Streets of Bangladesh Capitol," CNN.com, September 29, 2015, http://www.cnn.com/2015/09/29/asia/bangladesh-isis-italian-killed/index.html.

4. "EgyptAir Mechanic Suspected in Russian Plane Crash," Reuters, January 30, 2016, http://uk.reuters.com/article/us-egypt-crash-suspects-idUKKCN0V712V.

5. Tim Lister et al., "ISIS Goes Global," CNN.com, February 13, 2017, http://www.cnn.com/2015/12/17/world/mapping-isis-attacks-around-the-world/.

6. Henry Johnson, "Months After ISIS Attack Egypt's Tourism Industry Is Still Paying the Price," Foreign Policy (online), March 1, 2016, http://foreignpolicy.com/2016/03/01/months-after-isis-attack-egypts-tourism-industry-still-paying-the-price/.

7. Ben Popken, "Global Tourism Takes Massive Hit After Spike in Terror Attacks," NBCNEWS.com, July 21, 2016, http://www.nbcnews.com/business/travel/global-tourism-takes-massive-hit-after-spike-terror-attacks-n614111.

Chapter 8: Felling the Behemoth

1. Sun Tzu, *The Art of War*, translated by Lionel Giles, MIT.edu, http://classics.mit.edu/Tzu/artwar.html.

2. "Terror's New Headquarters," *Economist* (online), June 14, 2014, http://www.economist.com/news/leaders/21604160-iraqs-second-city-has-fallen-group-wants-create-state-which-wage-jihad.

3. Rick Gladstone, "Iraqi Forces Take Eastern Mosul from Islamic State," *New York Times* (online), January 18, 2017, https://www.nytimes.com/2017/01/18/world/middleeast/iraq-mosul-isis.html.

4. "Global Terrorism Index, 2015," Institute for Economics and Peace, http://economicsandpeace.org/wp-content/uploads/2015/11/Global-Terrorism-Index-2015.pdf.

5. Greg Miller and Julie Tate, "Osama bin Laden Warned Against Almost Every Aspect of Islamic State Playbook," *Washington Post* (online), March 1, 2016, https://www.washingtonpost.com/world/national-security/in-secret-will-bin-laden-wanted-his-fortune-to-keep-funding-war-on-west/2016/03/01/b3a03d6c-dfa4-11e5-846c-10191d1fc4cc_story.html?utm_term=.905cf942a9ef.

6. Kelsey D. Atherton, "IED Drone Kills Kurdish Soldiers, French Commandos," *Popular Science* (online), October 11, 2016, http://www.popsci.com/booby-trapped-isis-drone-kills-kurdish-soldiers-french-commandos.

7. Allen McDuffee, "DARPA Plans to Arm Drones with Missile-Blasting Lasers," *Wired* (online), November 1, 2013, https://www.wired.com/2013/11/drone-lasers.

8. J. M. Berger, "The Metronome of Apocalyptic Time: Social Media as a Carrier Wave for Millenarian Contagion," *Perspectives on Terrorism*, vol. 9, no. 4 (2015), p. 65.

9. J. M. Berger, "Taming ISIS on Twitter: More Than a Game of Whack-a-Mole," CNN.com, April 2, 2015, http://www.cnn.com/2015/03/13/opinions/isis-twitter-crackdown/.

GLOSSARY

Abu Bakr al-Baghdadi The leader of ISIS, Baghdadi helped found al-Qaeda in Iraq, which would later become ISIS. Prior to his complete radicalization, Baghdadi was detained by US forces at Camp Bucca in Iraq but was released in 2004. He has been serving as leader of the group now known as ISIS since 2010.

al-Qaeda A terrorist organization founded by Osama bin Laden and now run by Ayman al-Zawahiri, al-Qaeda is a militant Sunni group that was responsible for the September 11, 2001, attacks on the United States.

Boko Haram A terrorist organization based in Nigeria that has pledged allegiance and support to ISIS.

caliph A person who is considered to be a successor to the Muslim prophet Muhammad and the leader of the entire Muslim community.

caliphate A Muslim state that is governed by the laws of Islam and is run by a caliph. The caliphate run by ISIS is guided by Sharia law.

Hadith In Islam, a Hadith is a report of the actions and sayings of the prophet Muhammad. Second only to the Quran, the Hadith are based on stories told about the Prophet after his death.

hashtag On social media, hashtags are labels inserted after tweets or Instagram posts and allow users to view all posts on a specific topic. Hashtags are noted by the number sign (#) on social media.

Islam A religion that believes there is only one god, known as Allah, and that Muhammad is the final prophet. Islam is broken into a number of sects, much like Christianity is divided, and approximately 23 percent of the world follows this religion.

Islamic State Also called ISIS, ISIL, IS, or Da'esh, the Islamic State is a terror group that practices an extreme version of Islam and believes that Muslims should live in their own state, separate from the nonbelievers.

jihad In Arabic, *jihad* means "to strive" or "struggle," but in common usage it means "to fight a holy war for Islam."

Levant The Levant is a geographic region that covers parts of Europe, Asia, and Africa. Countries that make up the Levant are Cyprus, Israel, Iraq, Jordan, Lebanon, Palestine, Syria, and Turkey. ISIS, which does not believe in modern geographic borders, refers specifically to regions of Syria and Iraq as the Levant.

lone wolf Someone who acts on his or her own without being specifically ordered by a leader or group. In terms of terrorism, a lone wolf is an attacker who chooses and carries out his or her own attack in the name of ISIS but who is not directed to do so by ISIS leaders and does not receive support from the greater ISIS organization.

Muhammad The Prophet, or messenger from God, in the Islamic faith, as well as the de facto founder of Islam. Muhammad lived in the seventh century, and in 610 CE, he reported receiving a visit from the angel Gabriel, who delivered to him the word of God.

mujahideen People engaged in jihad. ISIS fighters can be referred to as mujahideen.

Muslims Followers of the Islamic faith.

Osama bin Laden The founder of al-Qaeda, a terrorist group based in Afghanistan, from which ISIS originally grew. Bin Laden was responsible for the September 11, 2001, attacks on the United States. He was later captured and killed by US military forces in 2011.

Quran The Islamic holy book. It is believed that the Quran is the word of God as told to Muhammad and written down by Muhammad's scribes.

radicalization The process by which someone adopts an extreme political, social, or religious ideology. Radicalization requires outside influence, whether from a friend or family member, religious leader, or website.

Sharia law Islamic law derived from the writings in the Quran.

Soviet Union A collection of European states, led by Communist Russia, that existed from 1922 until 1991.

Sunna A collection of the teachings of Muhammad and one of the sources of Sharia, or Islamic law.

Taliban An extremist Muslim political group that forces followers to obey Sharia law.

West "The West" is a catchall phrase used mostly to mean America, but that also includes Europe and Canada. The name is derived from "Western Hemisphere," where America and Europe are located. As it regards ISIS, the West is the enemy of the caliphate.

FURTHER READING

Books

Fishman, Brian H. *The Master Plan: ISIS, al-Qaeda, and the Jihadi Strategy for Final Victory*. New Haven, CT: Yale University Press, 2016.

January, Brendan. *ISIS: The Global Face of Terrorism*. Minneapolis, MN: Twenty-First Century Books, 2017.

Kennan, Caroline. *The Rise of ISIS: The Modern Age of Terrorism*. Farmington Hills, MI: Lucent Press, 2017.

Wood, Graeme. *The Way of the Strangers*. New York, N.Y.: Random House, 2017.

Websites

Belfer Center
www.belfercenter.org

Run by Harvard's Kennedy School for Science and International Affairs, the Belfer Center offers detailed analysis on terrorism and war, not just in the United States, but around the globe.

New York Times
www.nytimes.com

This daily news website follows the news closely to allow you to keep up to date with what is happening in ISIS territory as well as with ISIS-inspired and ISIS-directed incidents around the world.

RAND

www.rand.org

A research organization, RAND studies terrorism and counterterrorism among other homeland security issues. Expert analysts offer commentary on not only the big picture of ISIS, but on recent incidents and attacks as well.

US Department of Homeland Security

www.dhs.gov

The US Department of Homeland Security offers up-to-the-minute news on security and terrorism issues facing the United States, as well as discussions about these topics from experts, politicians, and security officers.

INDEX